DON'T let the CAT eat the CAKE!

Belle Ange Designs

WRITTEN & ILLUSTRATED BY LINDA CAMPBELL

for Elena and Alethea

First published 2023
This edition published 2023, 002
Text copyright Linda Campbell
The moral right of the author has been asserted
With thanks to Conarsa Studio, Leamsign & Larysa Zabrotskaya

Printed by Amazon Kindle Publishing

ISBN 9798396990388

Now this is REALLY IMPORTANT so listen carefully. Whatever happens when I'm away, please PLEASE don't let the cat eat any of the cakes!

NOT. EVEN. ONE.

Mmmm now which cake should I eat first? How about a donut?

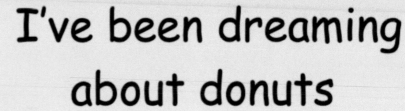

What do you mean, No?!

I thought we were friends.

How about

a cupcake?

Oh, come on! Cupcakes are my favourite!

C'mon you can't deny the shades are awesome!

I'm back!

I hope the cat didn't give you too much trouble.

You didn't let him eat cake did you?

Well done!
I knew you could do it!
Give yourself a high five!
And thank you.

YOU

ARE

HIRED!

Made in United States
Troutdale, OR
11/23/2023